A MIDSUMMER-NIGHT'S DREAM

BY WILLIAM SHAKESPEARE

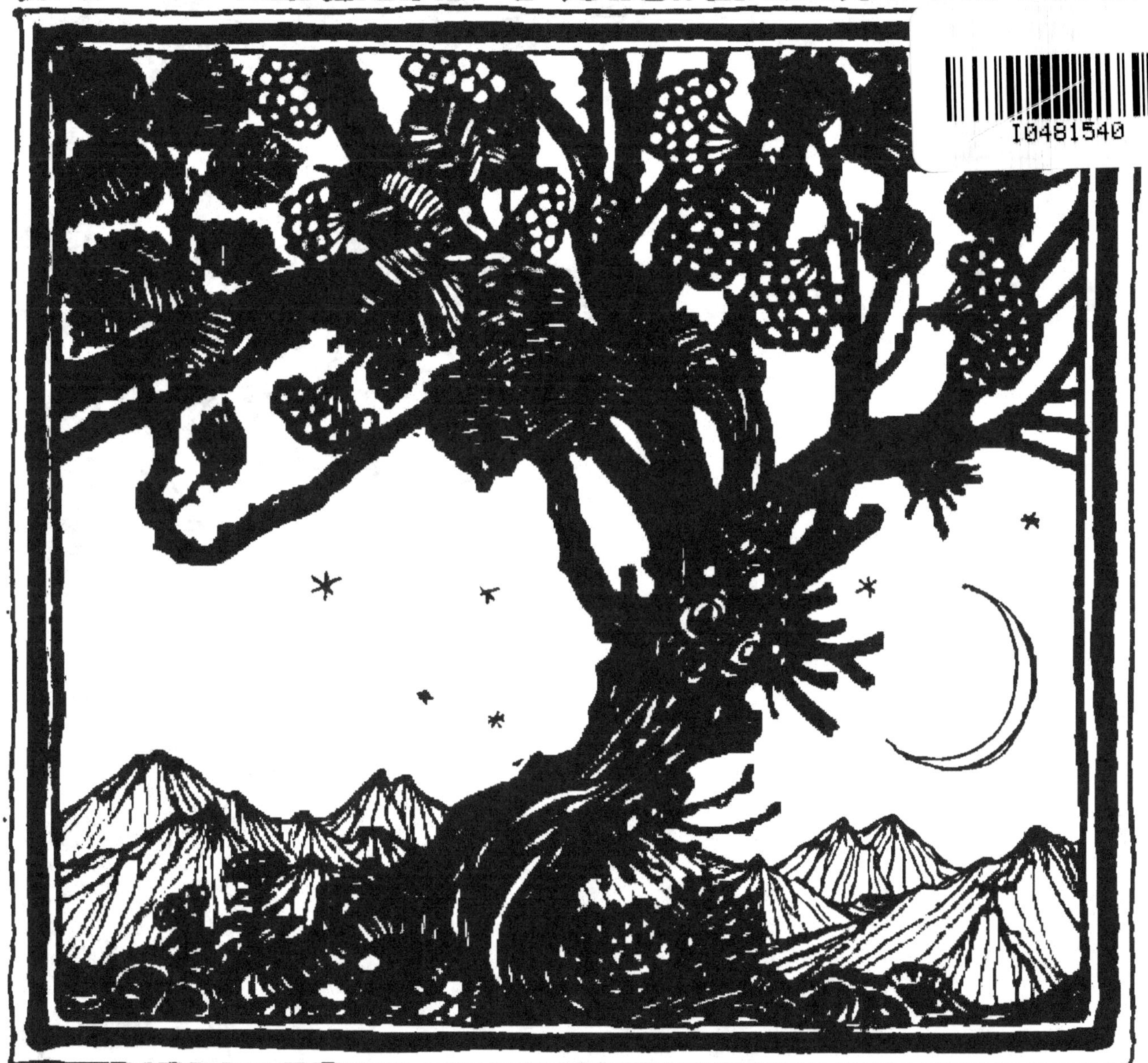

WITH ILLUSTRATIONS BY ARTHUR RACKHAM

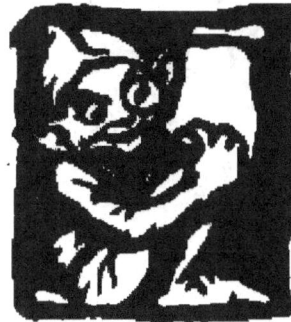

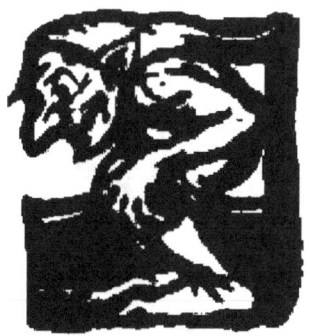

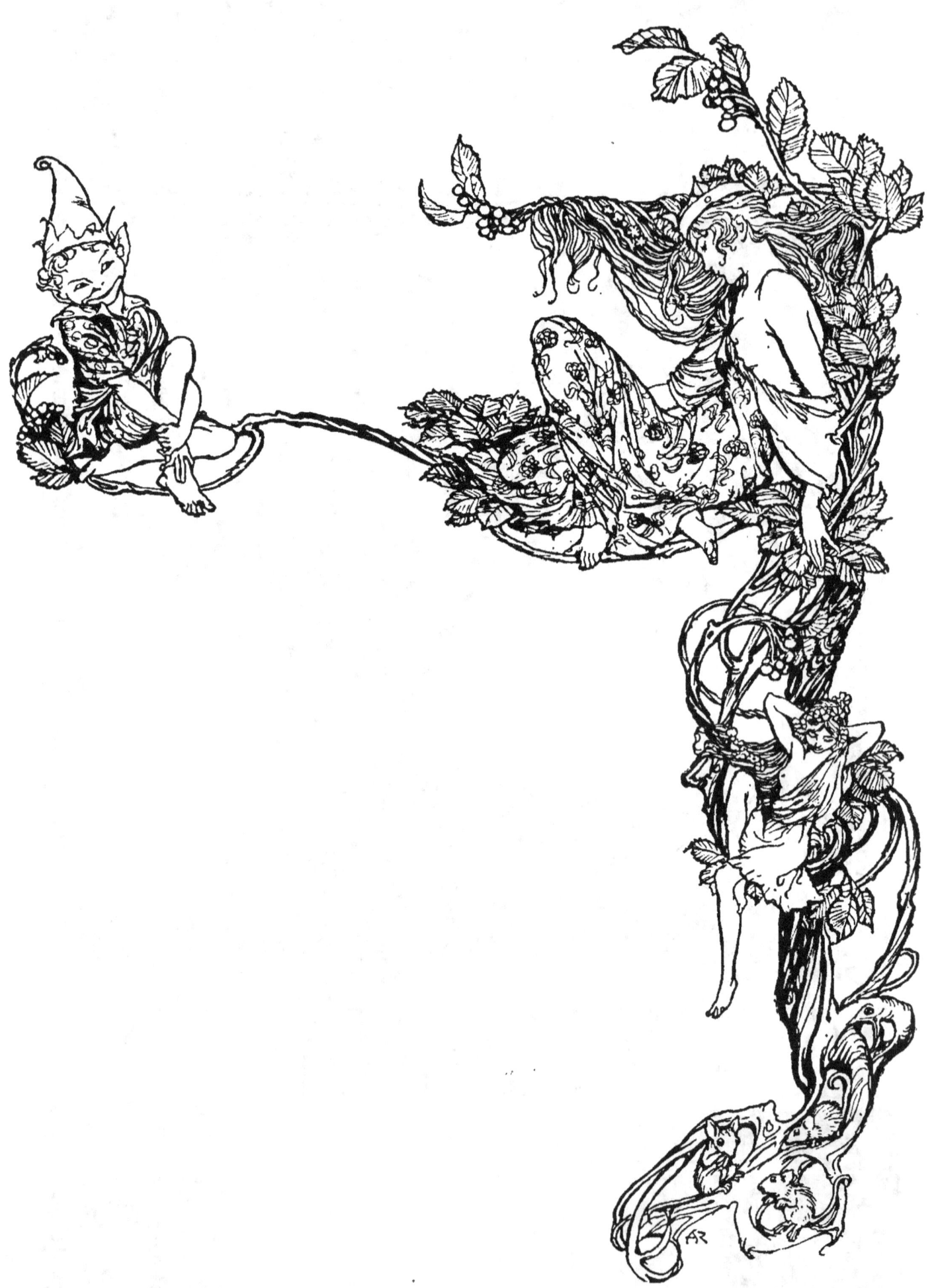

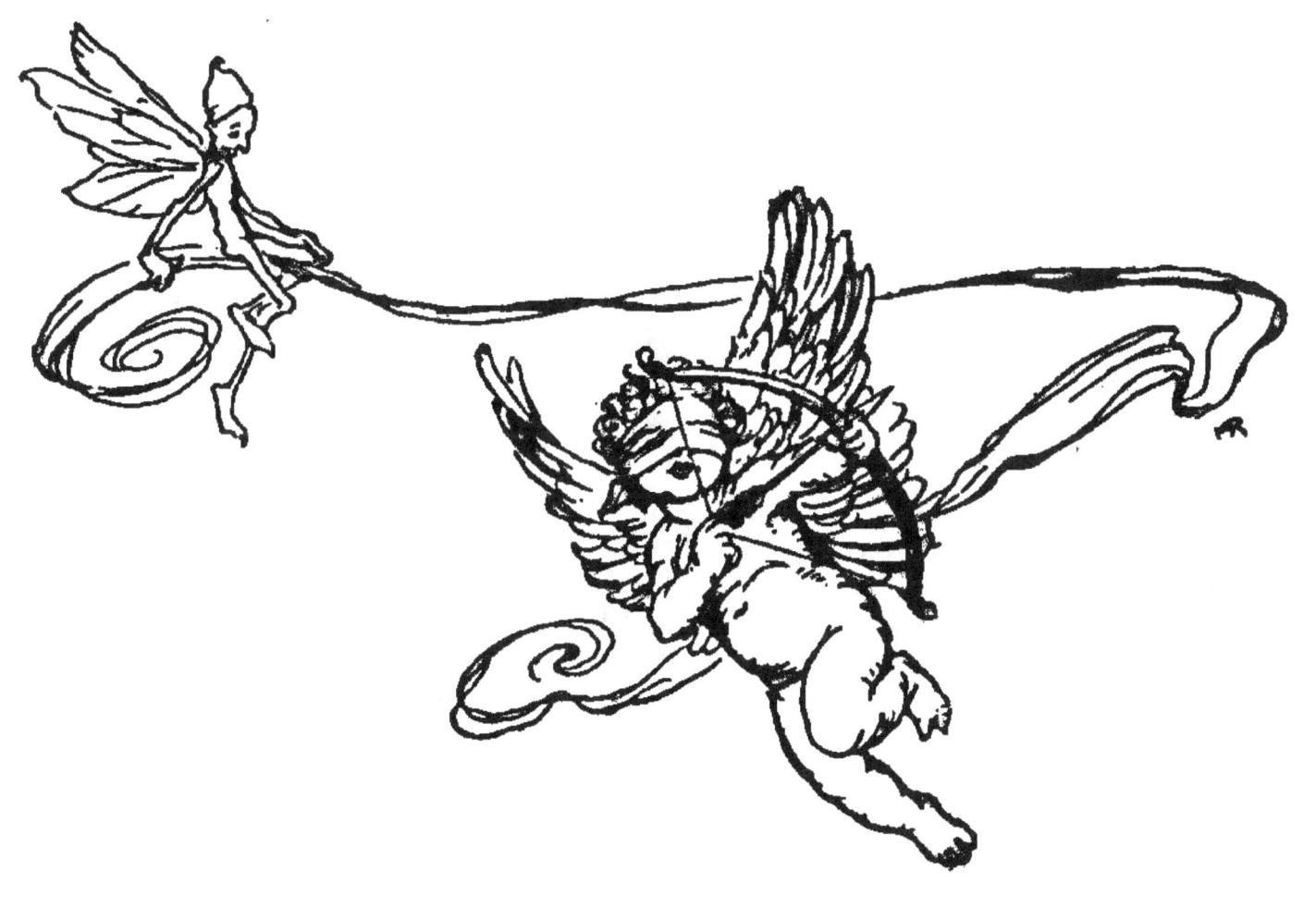

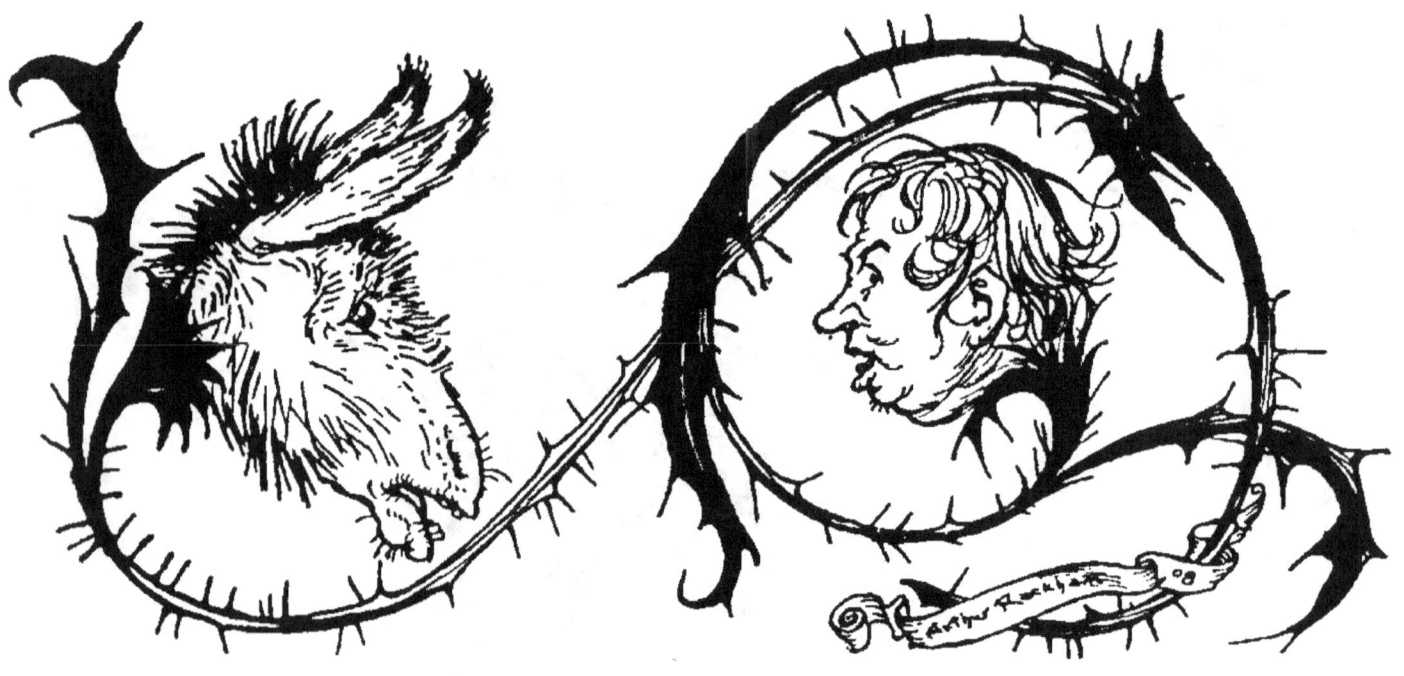

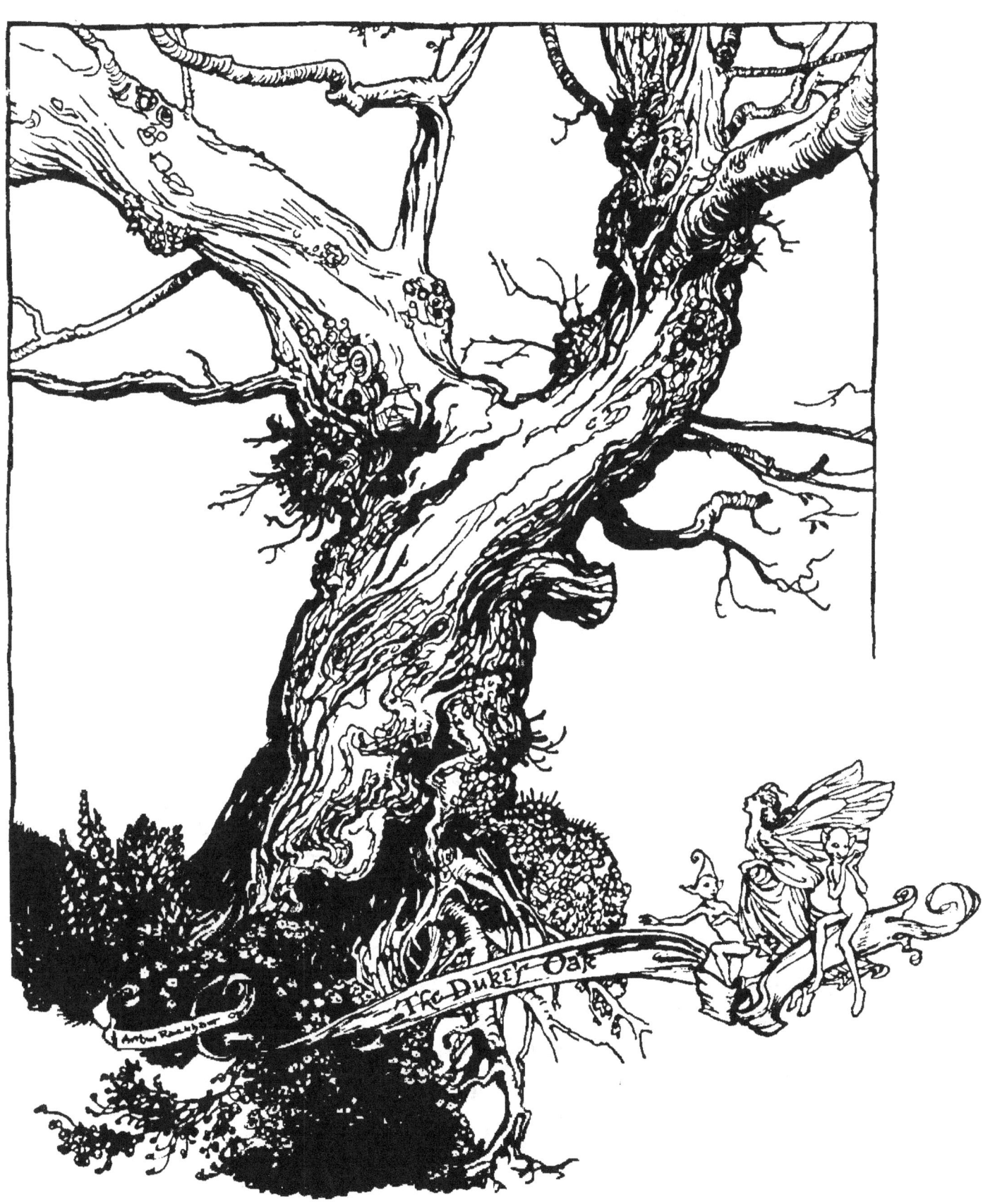

The Duke's Oak

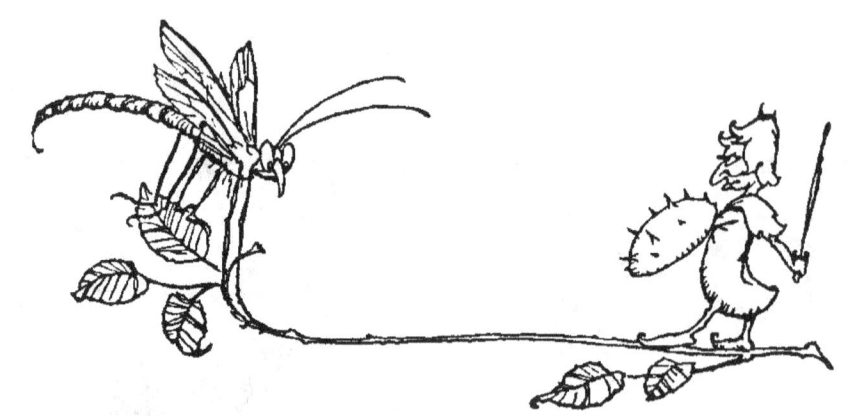

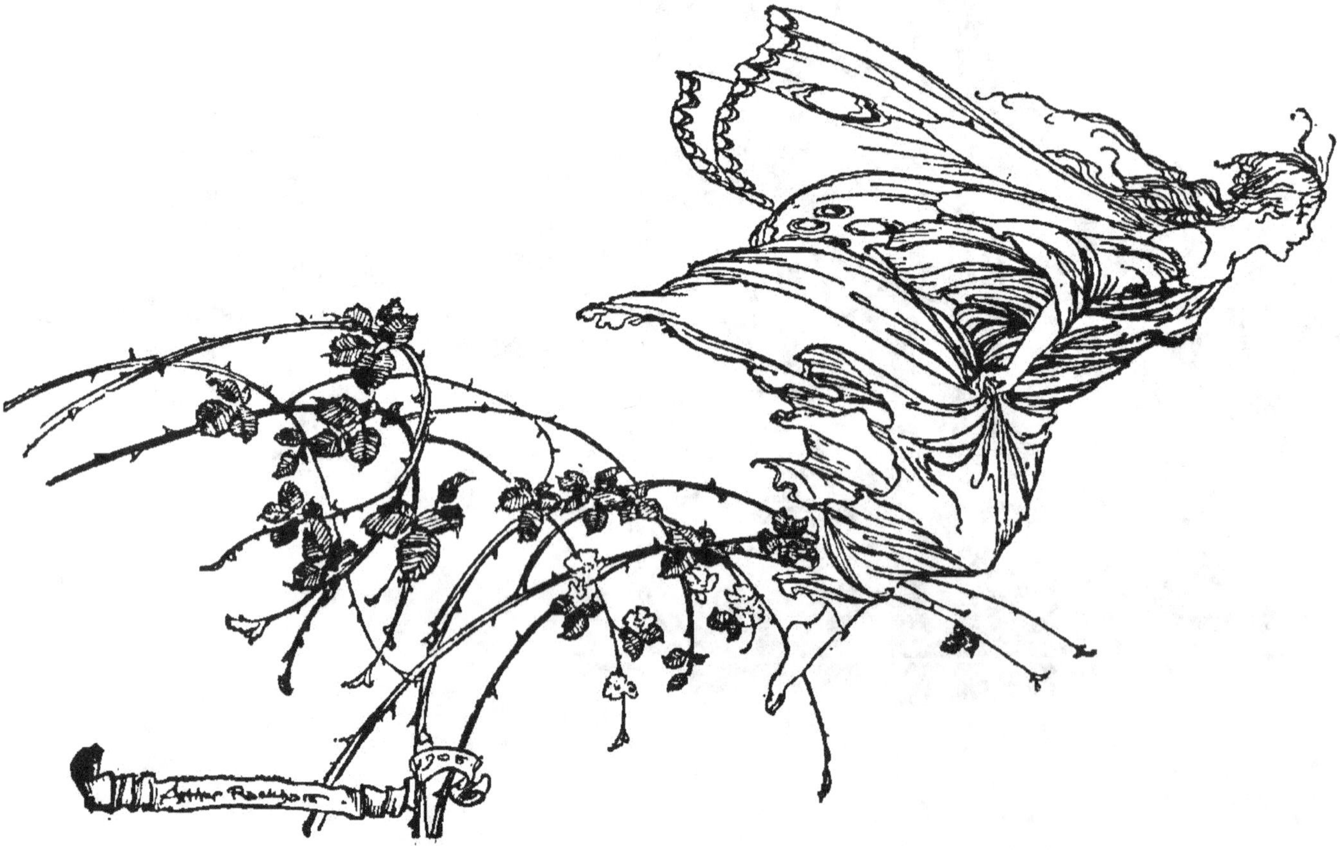

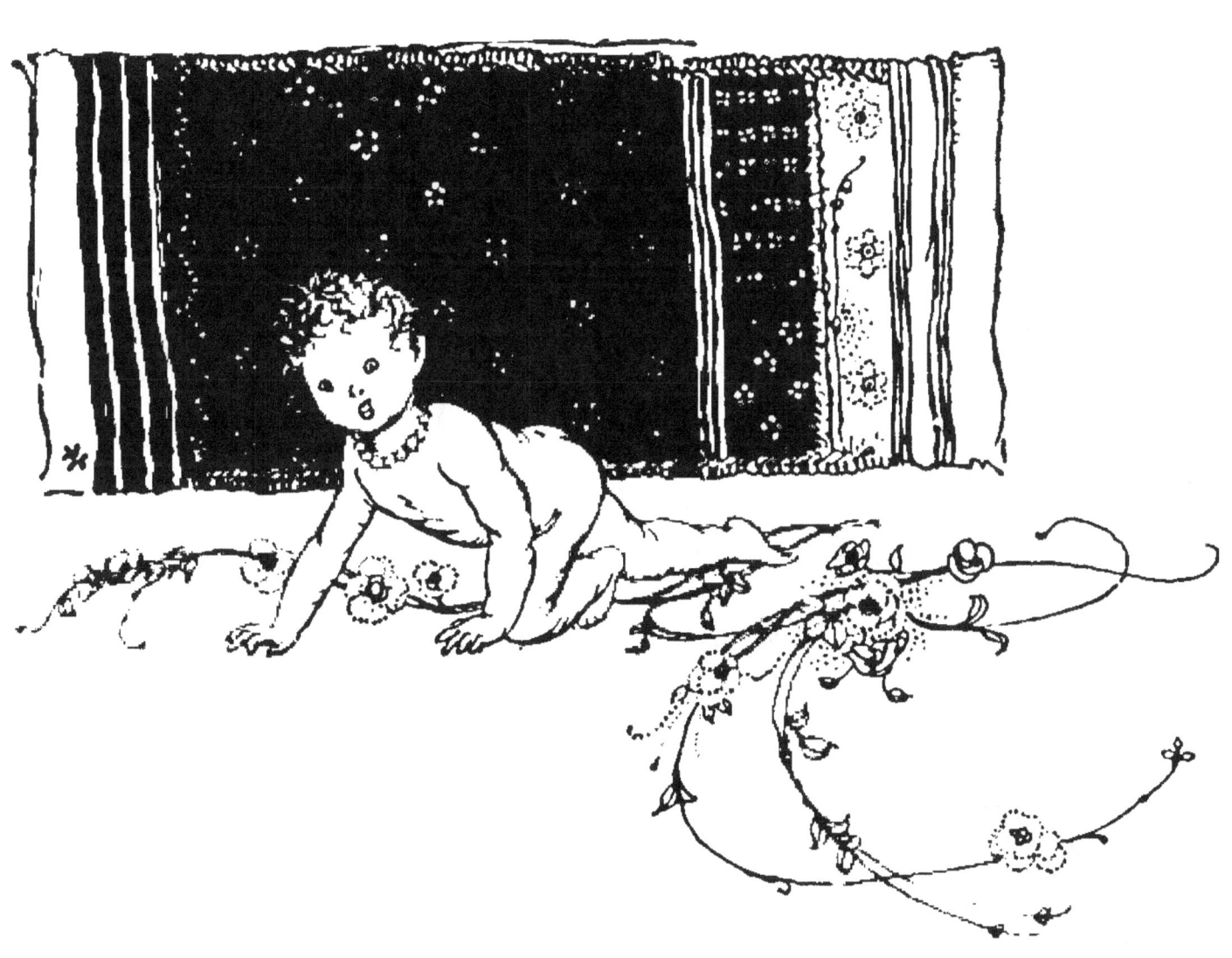

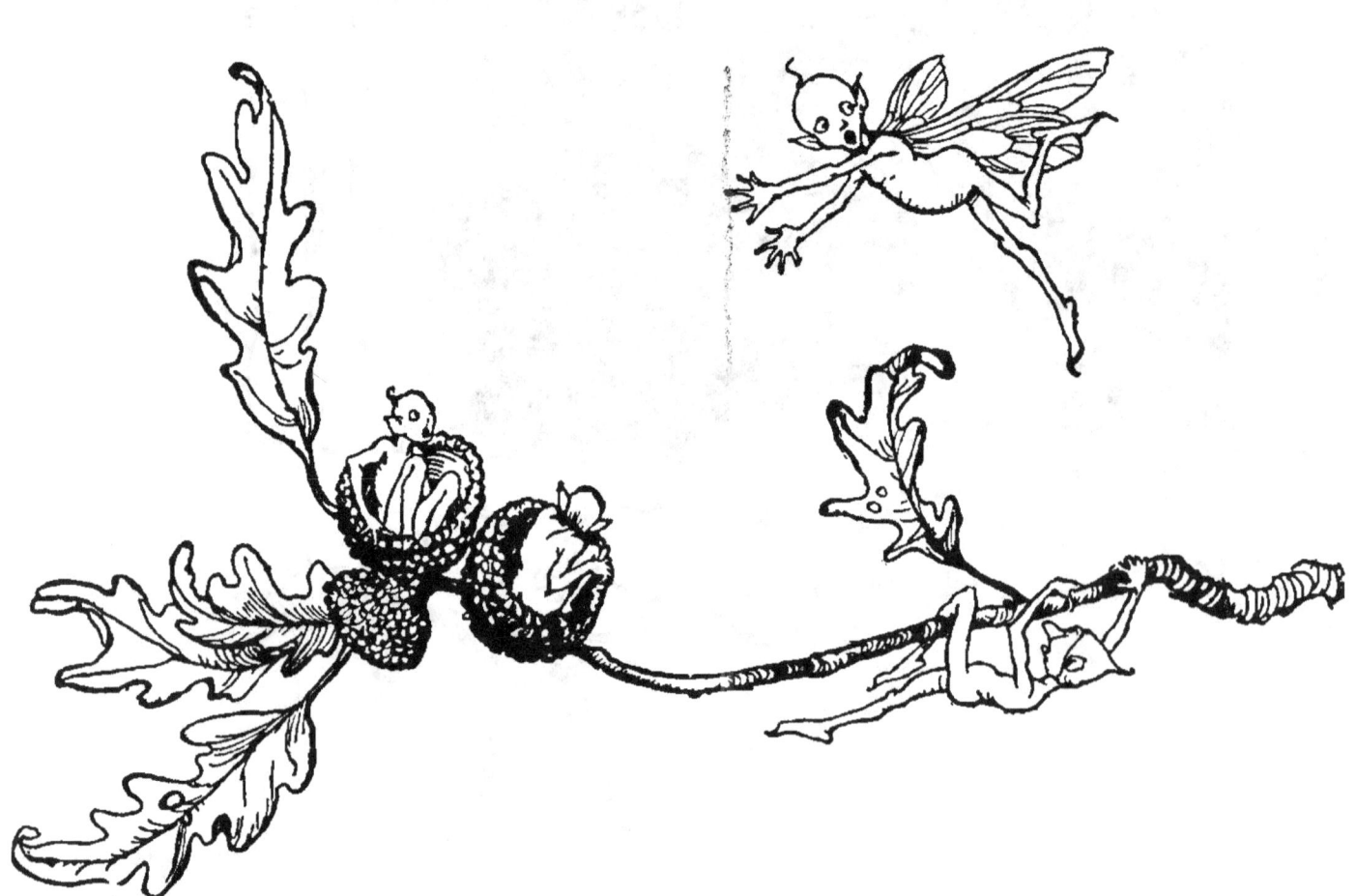

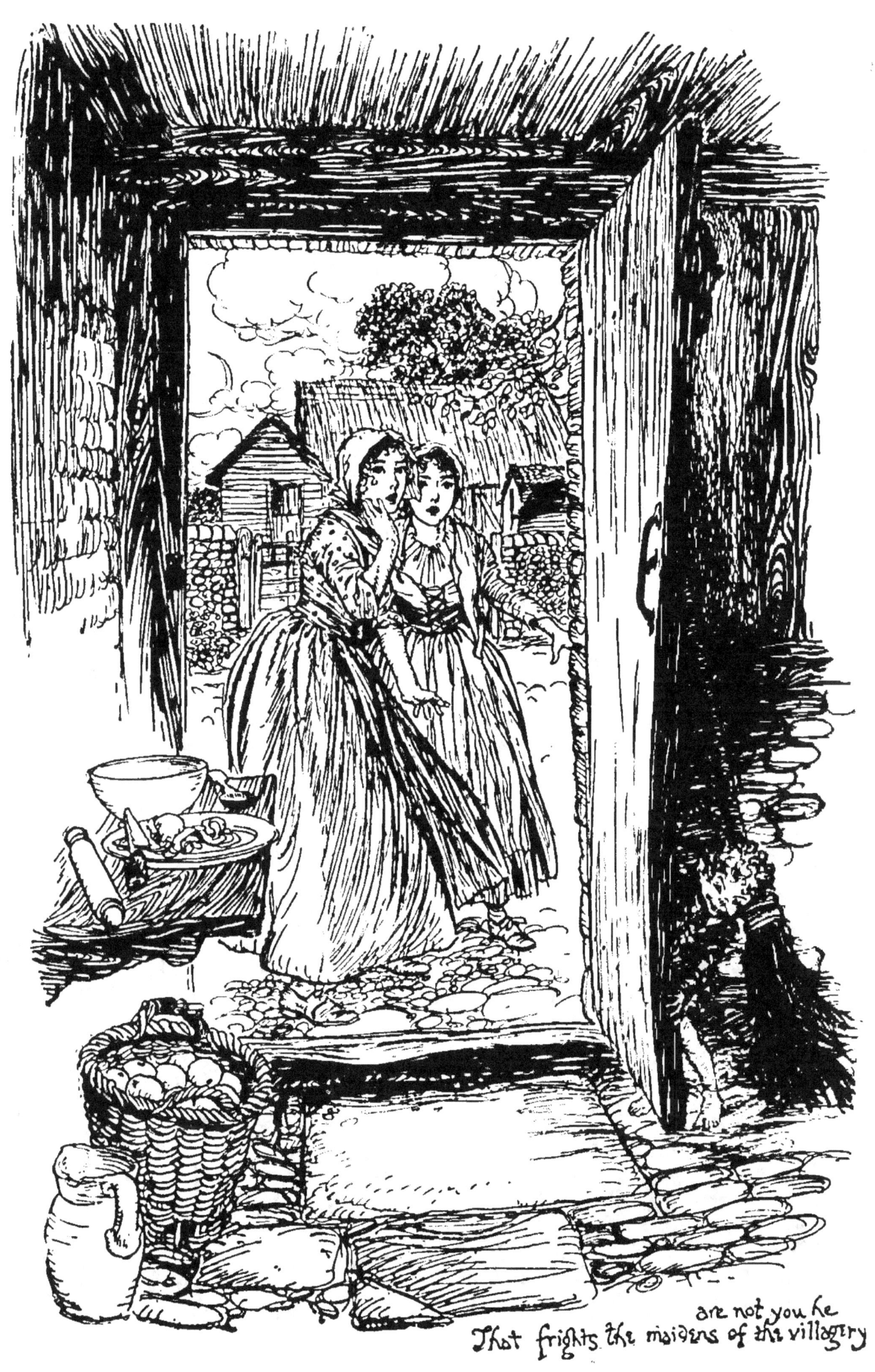

are not you he
That frights the maidens of the villagery

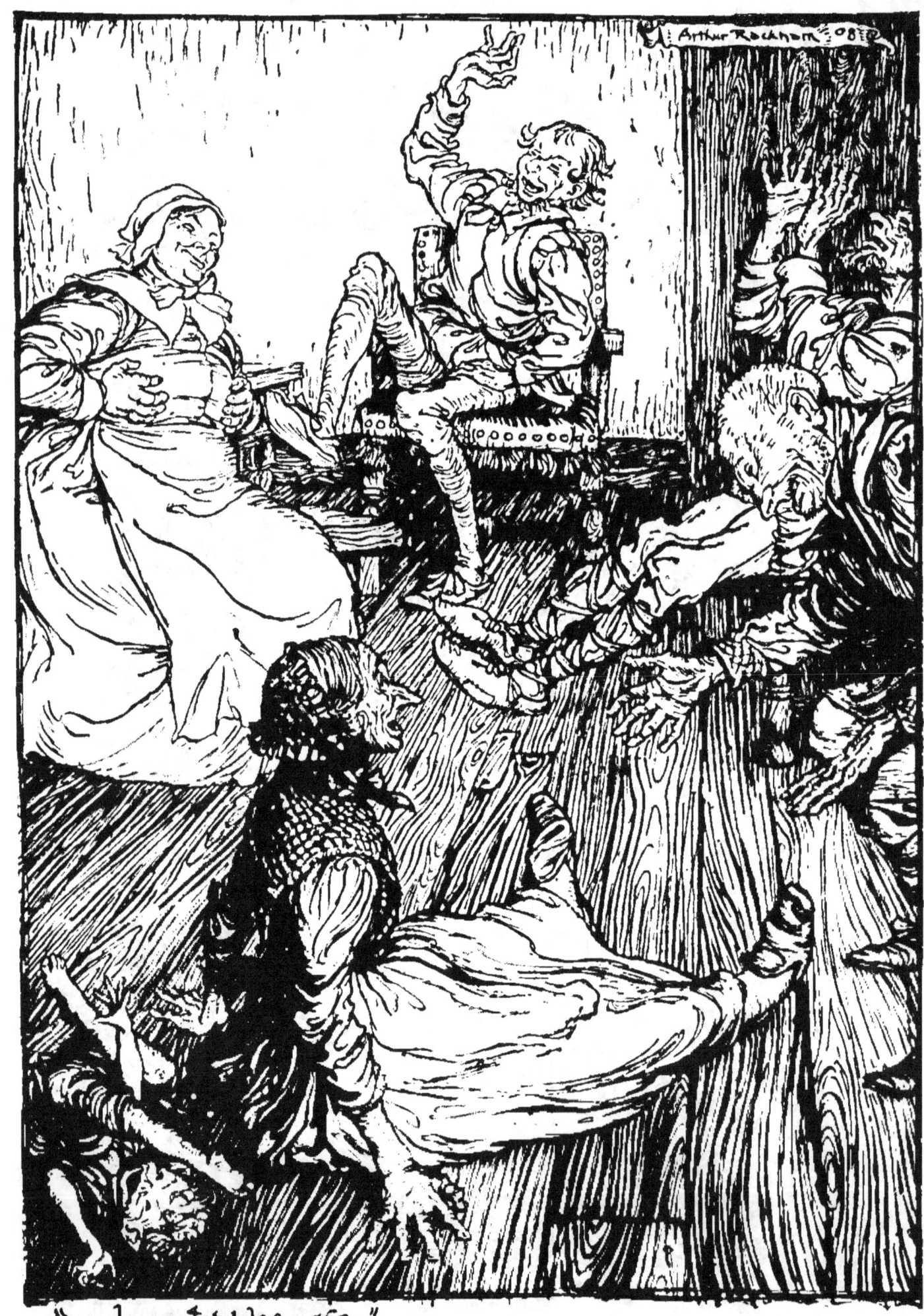

"— down topples she,"

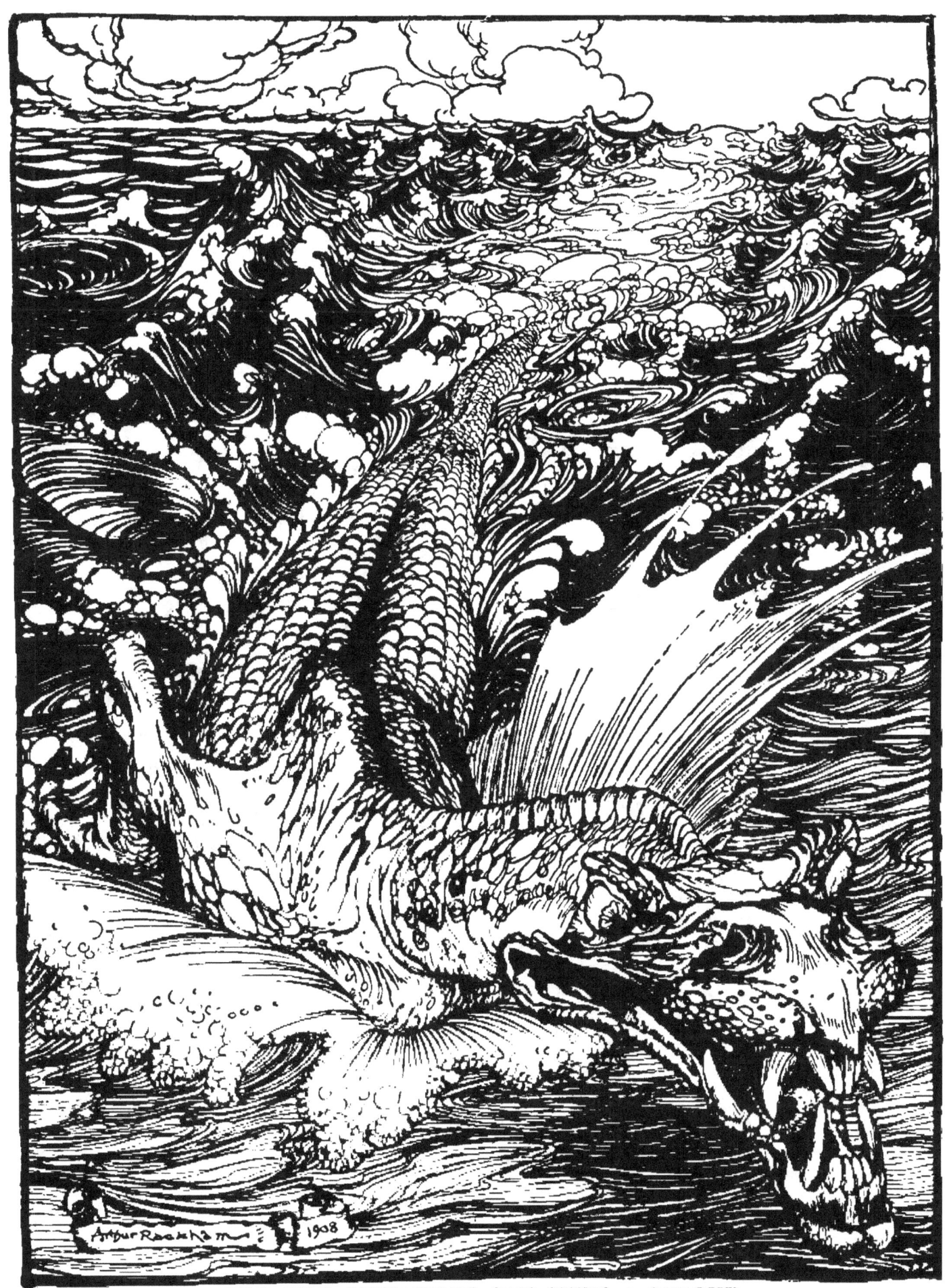

ERE THE LEVIATHAN CAN SWIM A LEAGUE

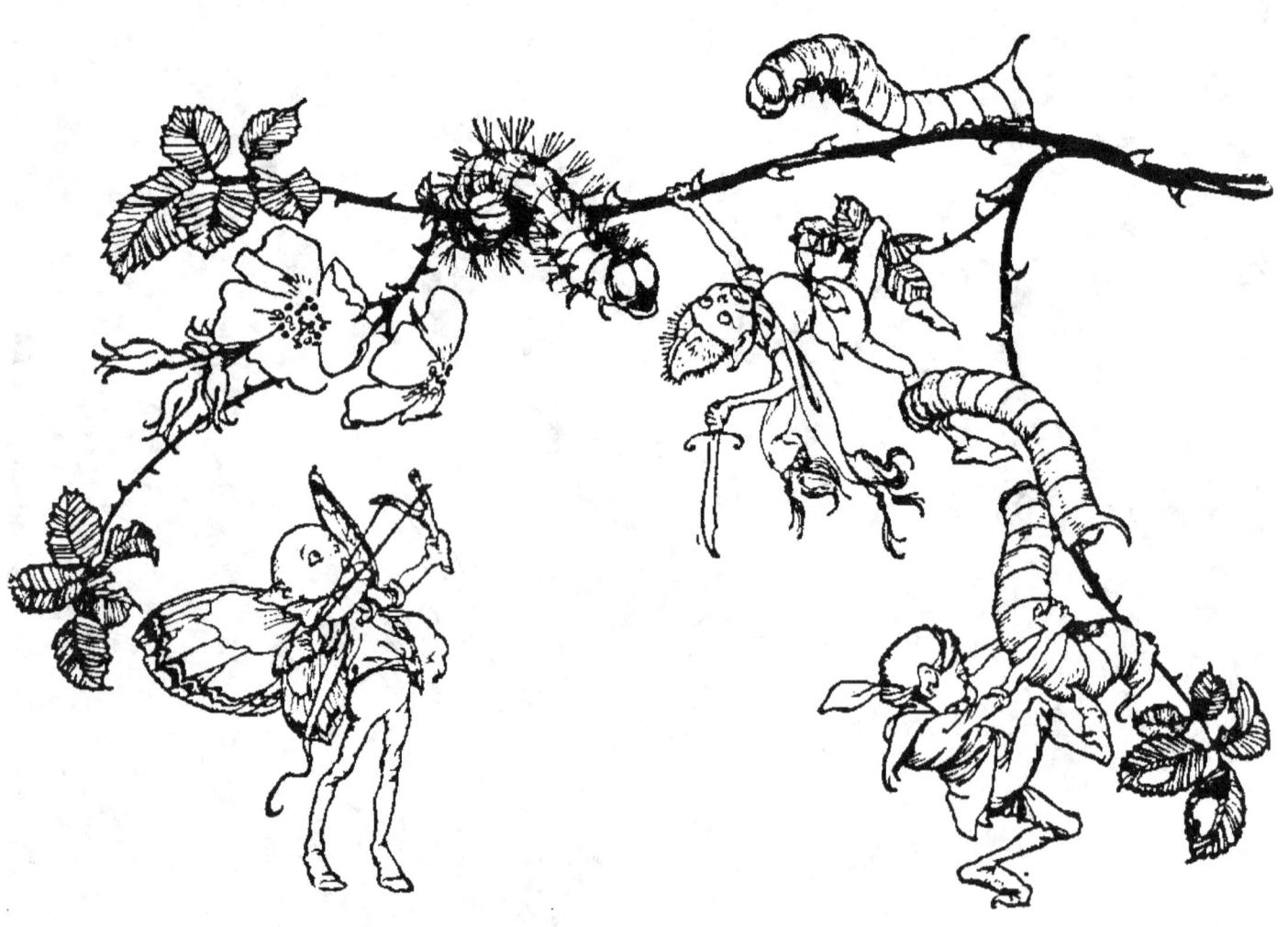

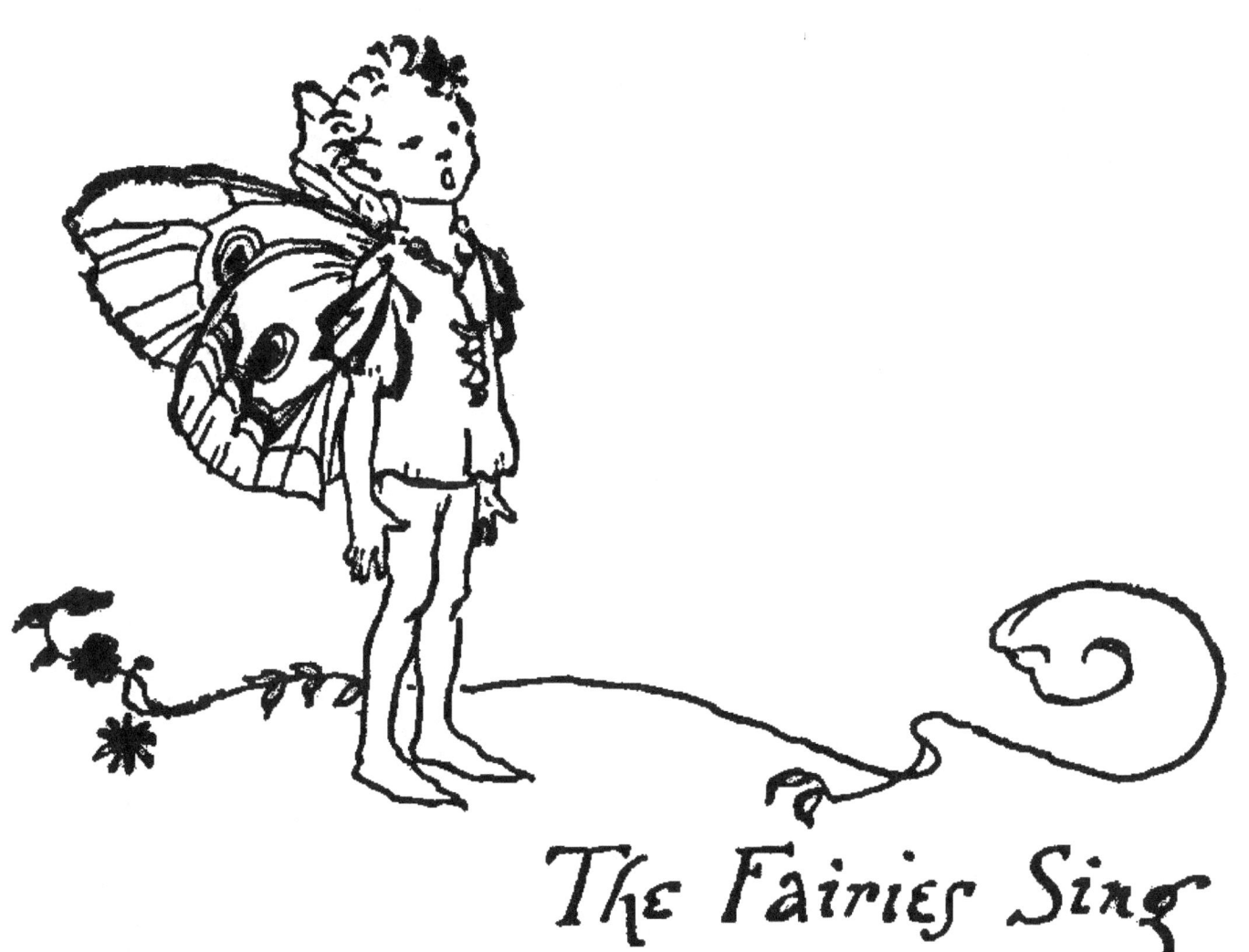

The Fairies Sing

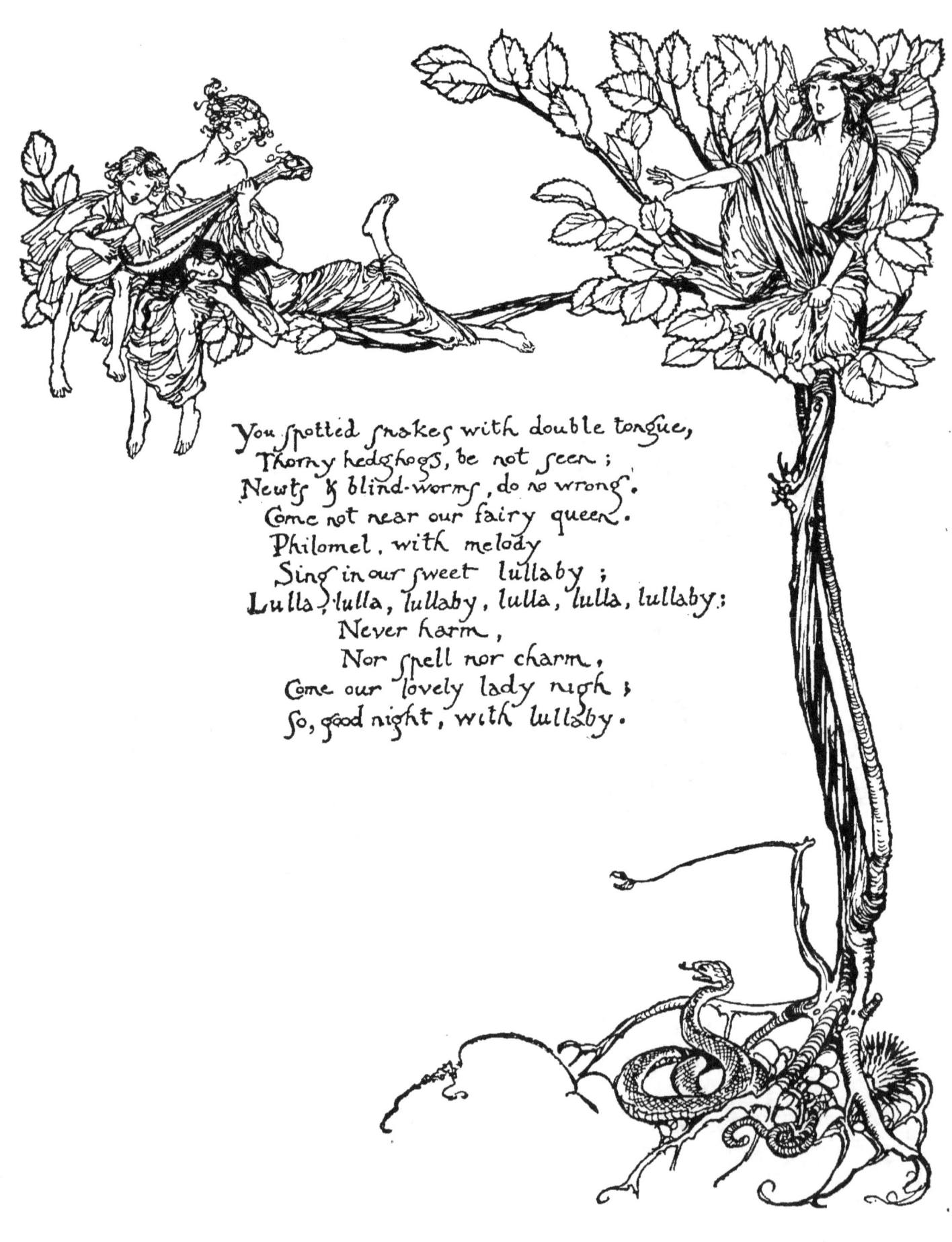

You spotted snakes with double tongue,
Thorny hedgehogs, be not seen;
Newts & blind-worms, do no wrong,
Come not near our fairy queen.
Philomel, with melody
Sing in our sweet lullaby;
Lulla, lulla, lullaby, lulla, lulla, lullaby:
Never harm,
Nor spell nor charm,
Come our lovely lady nigh;
So, good night, with lullaby.

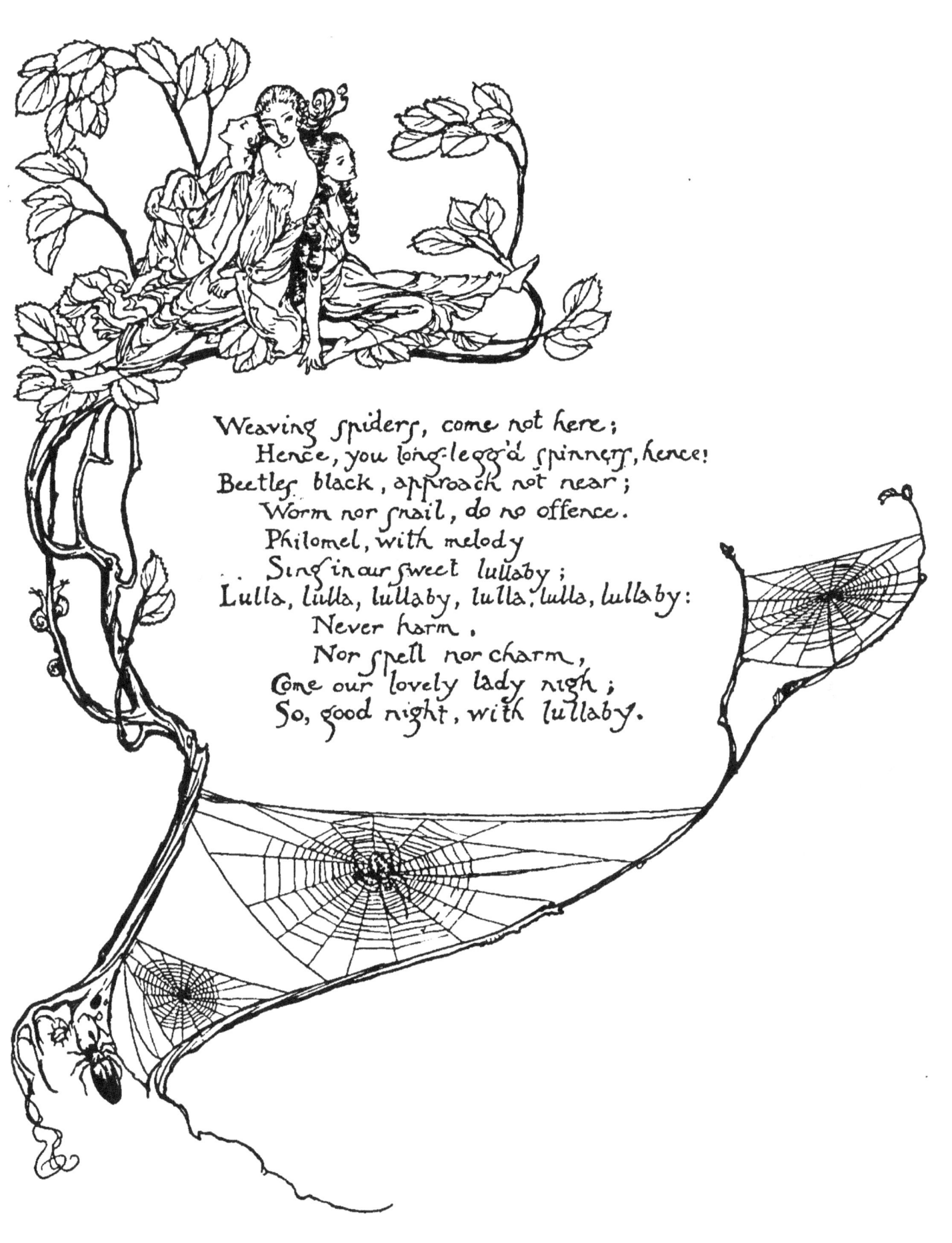

Weaving spiders, come not here;
 Hence, you long-legg'd spinners, hence!
Beetles black, approach not near;
 Worm nor snail, do no offence.
 Philomel, with melody
 Sing in our sweet lullaby;
Lulla, lulla, lullaby, lulla, lulla, lullaby:
 Never harm.
 Nor spell nor charm,
Come our lovely lady nigh;
 So, good night, with lullaby.

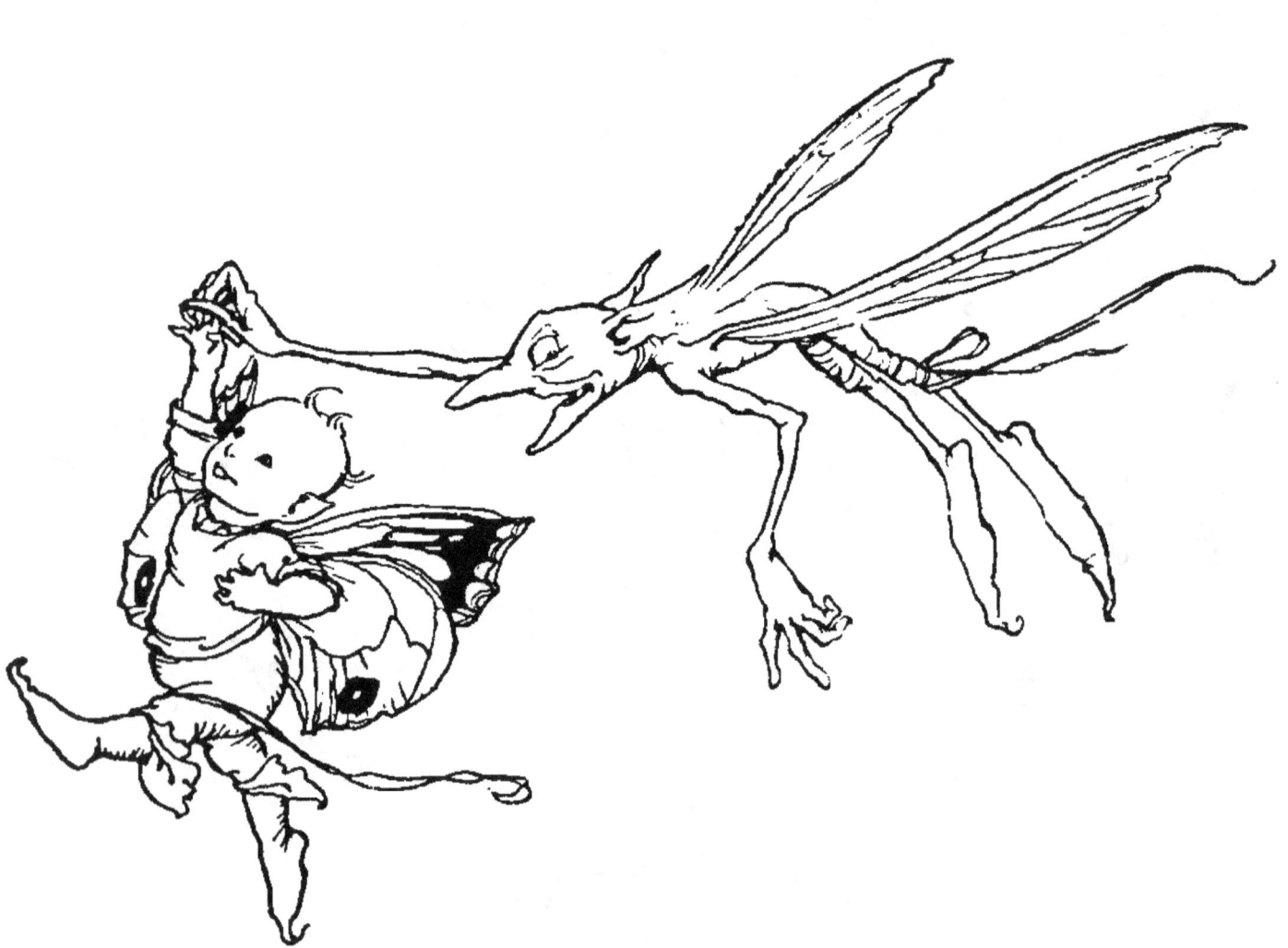

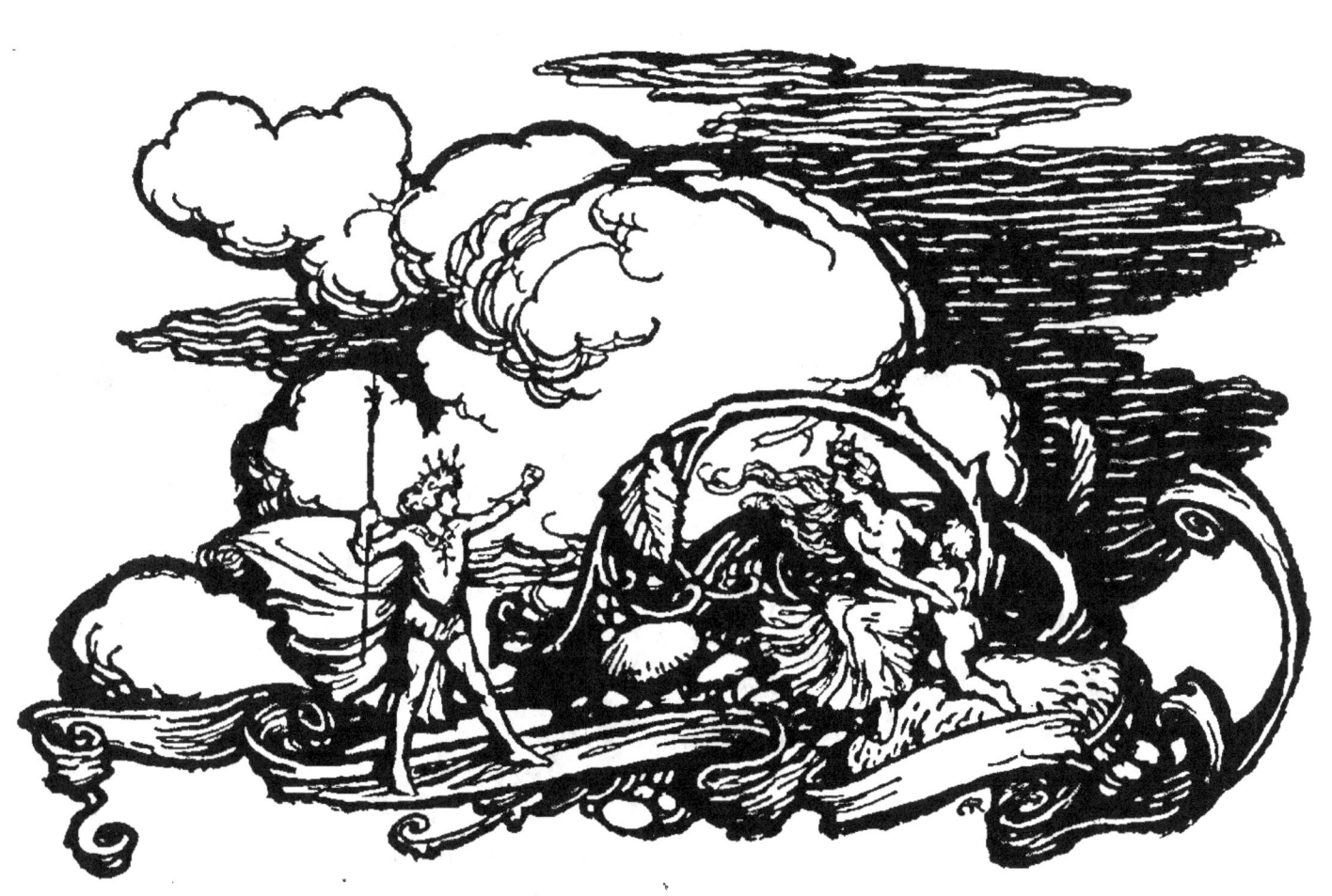

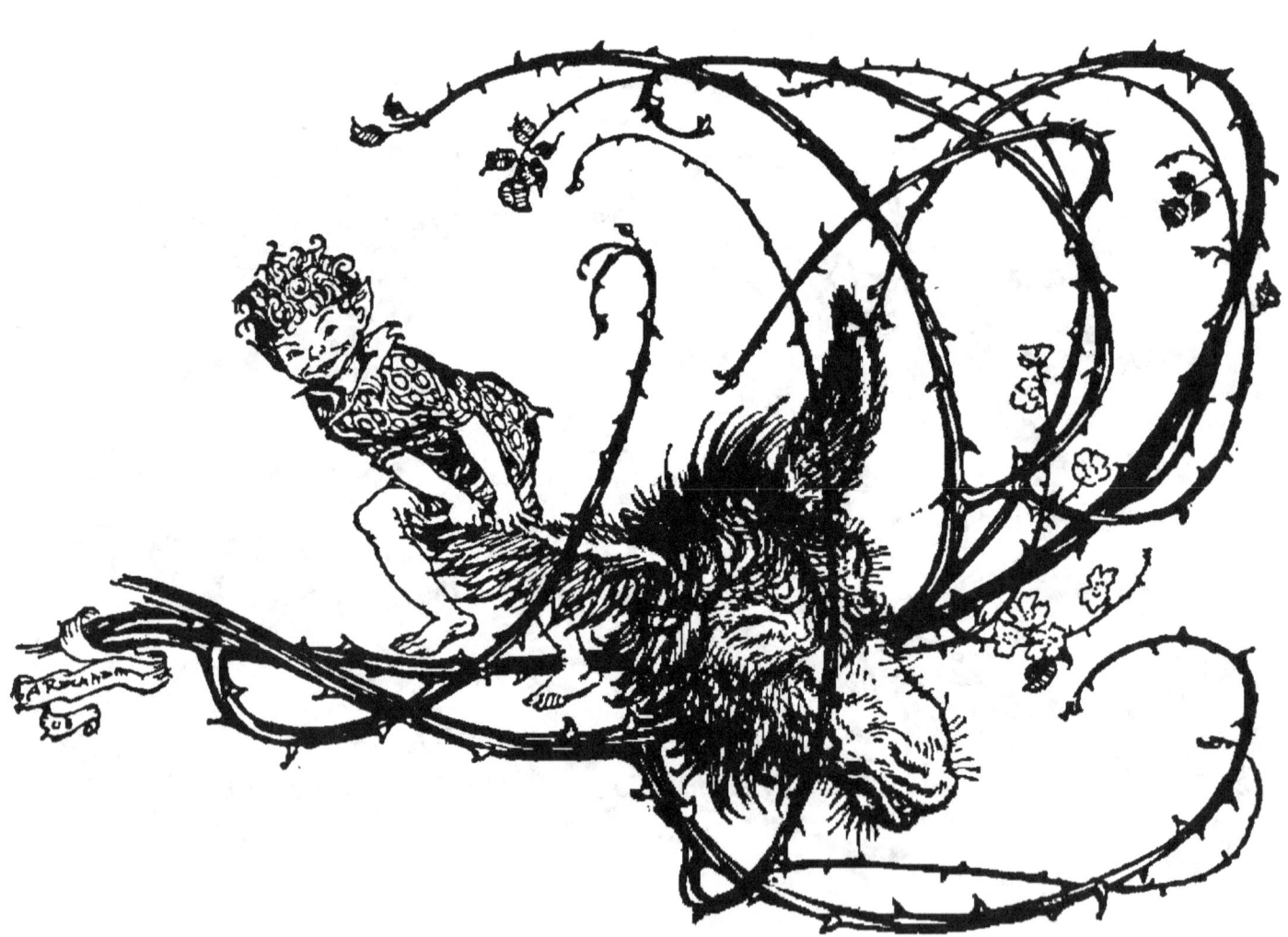

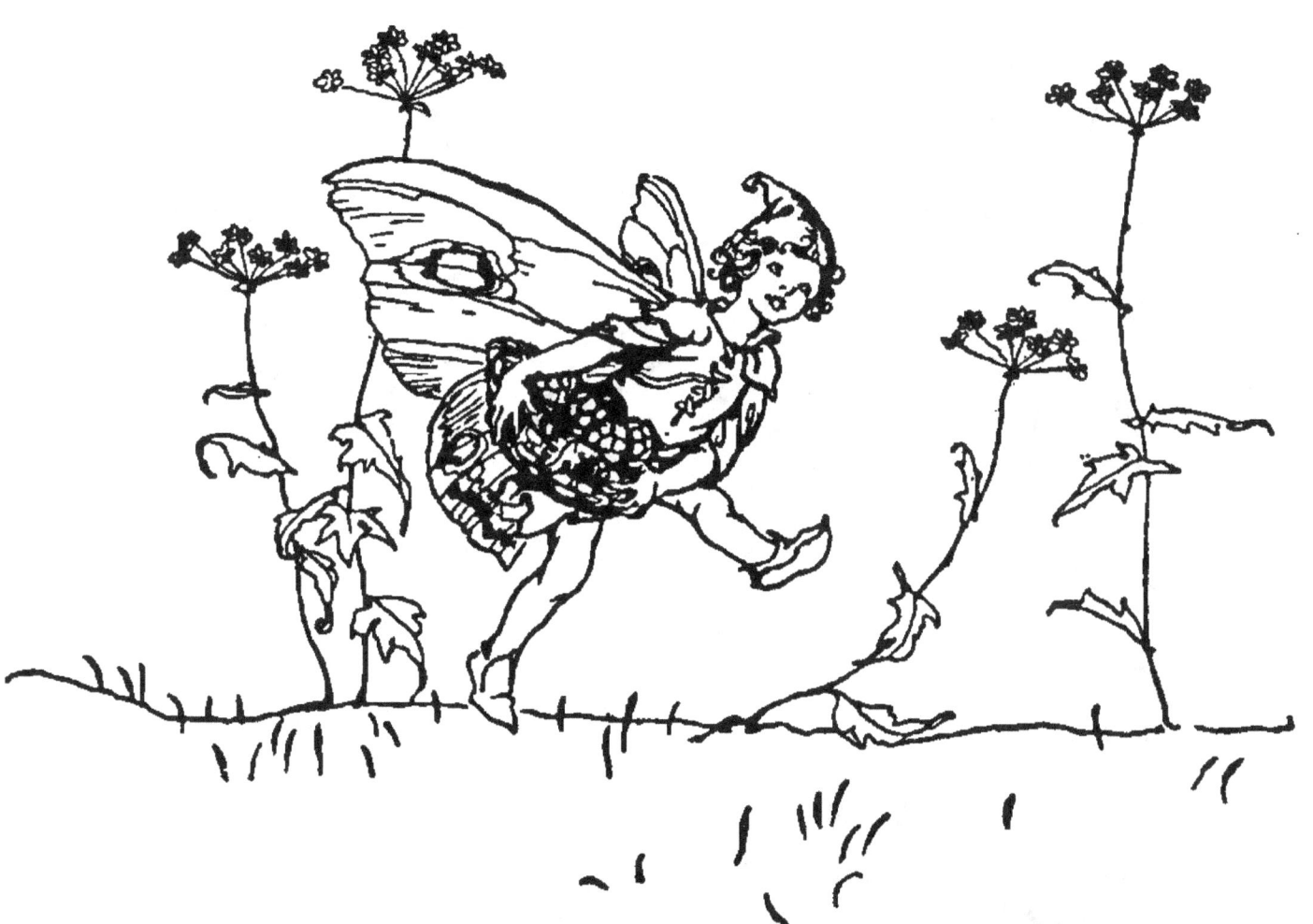

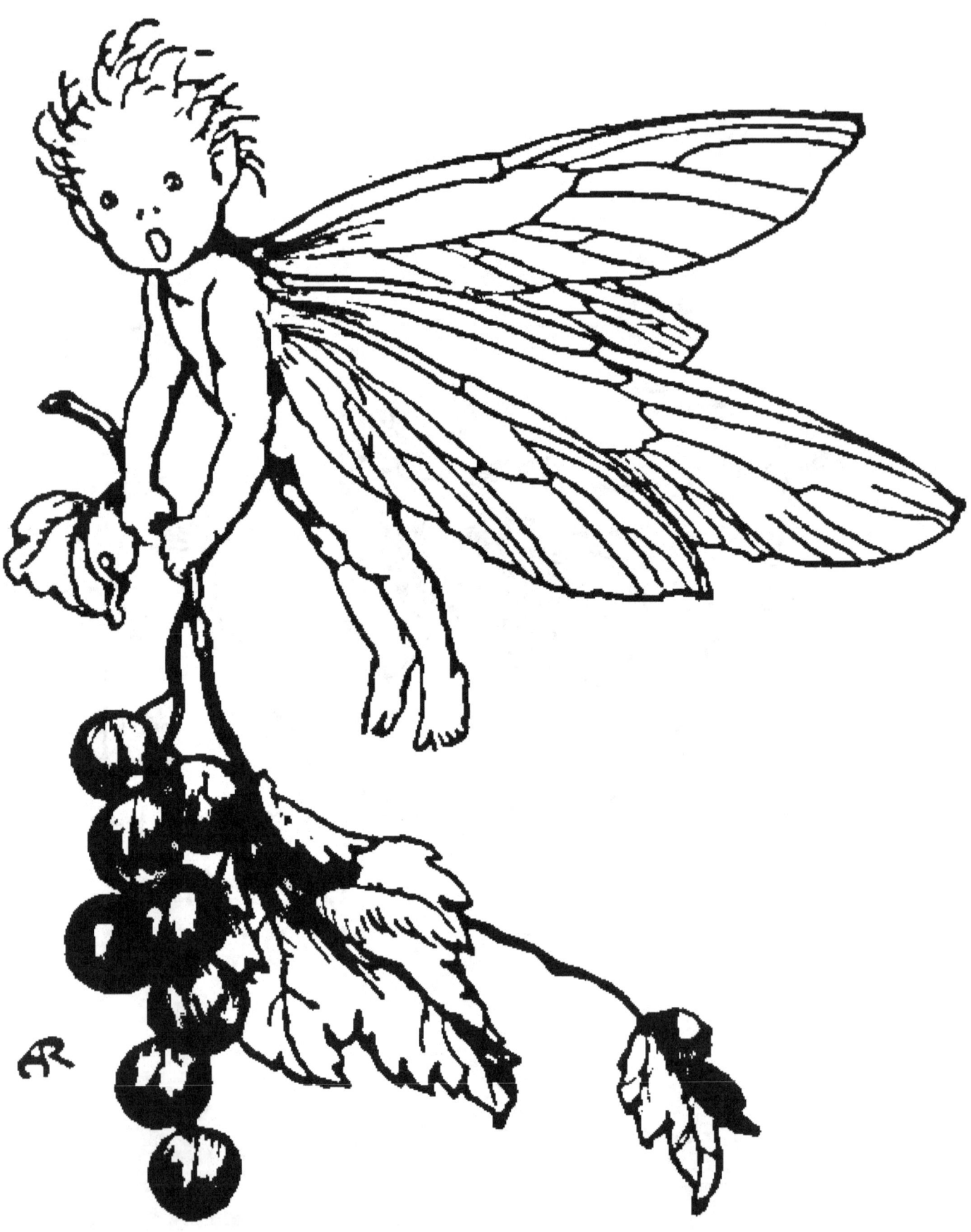

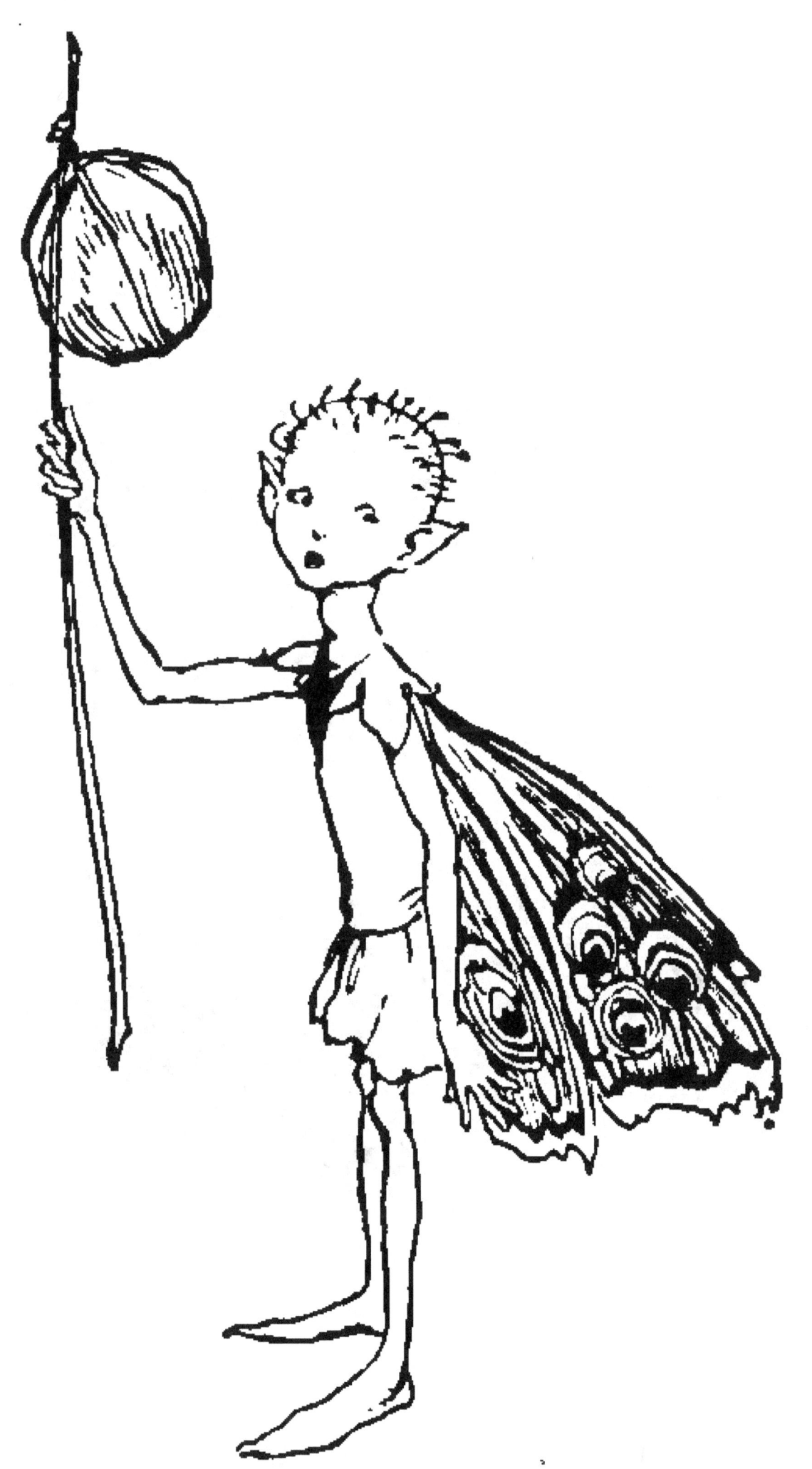

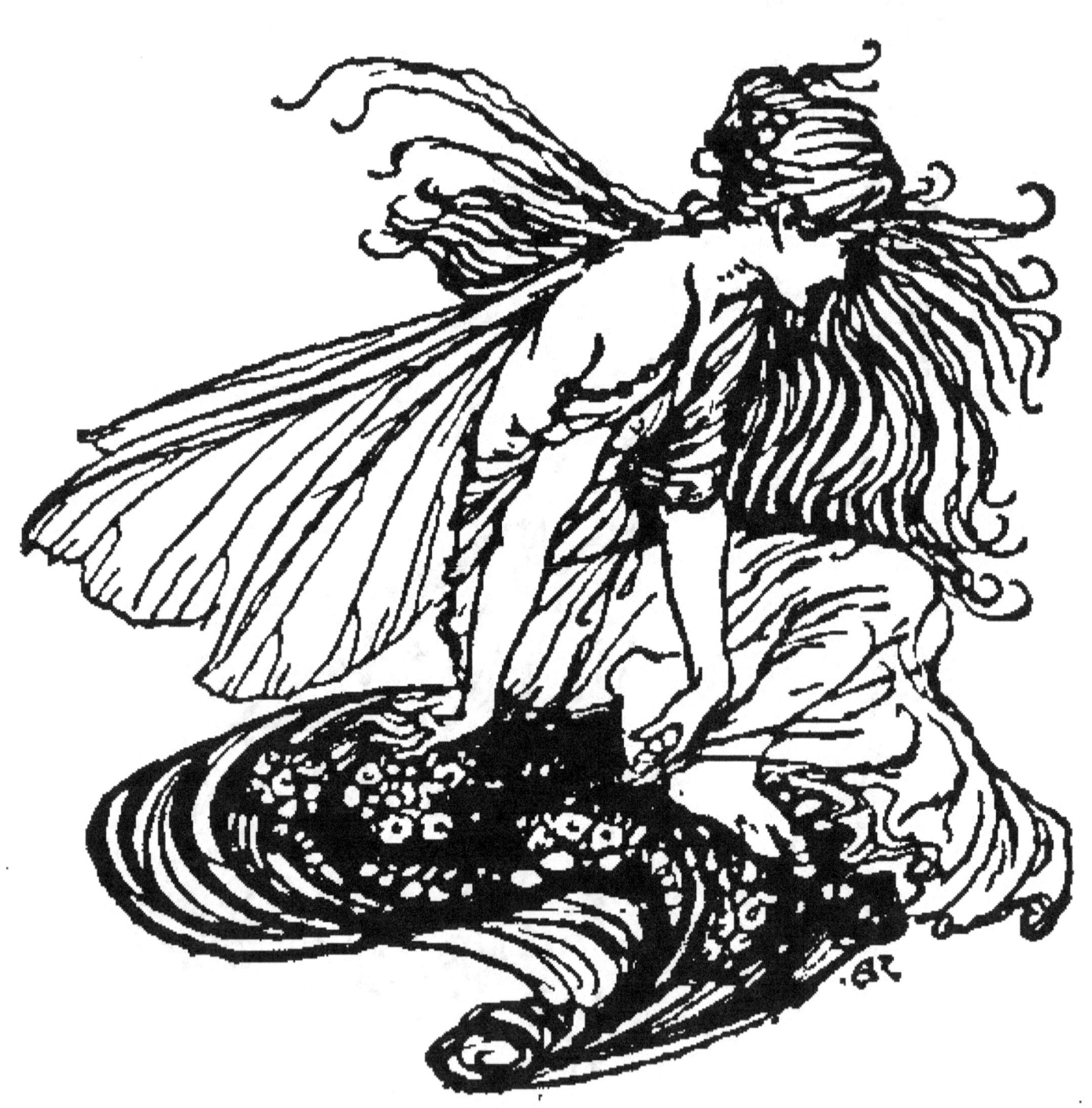

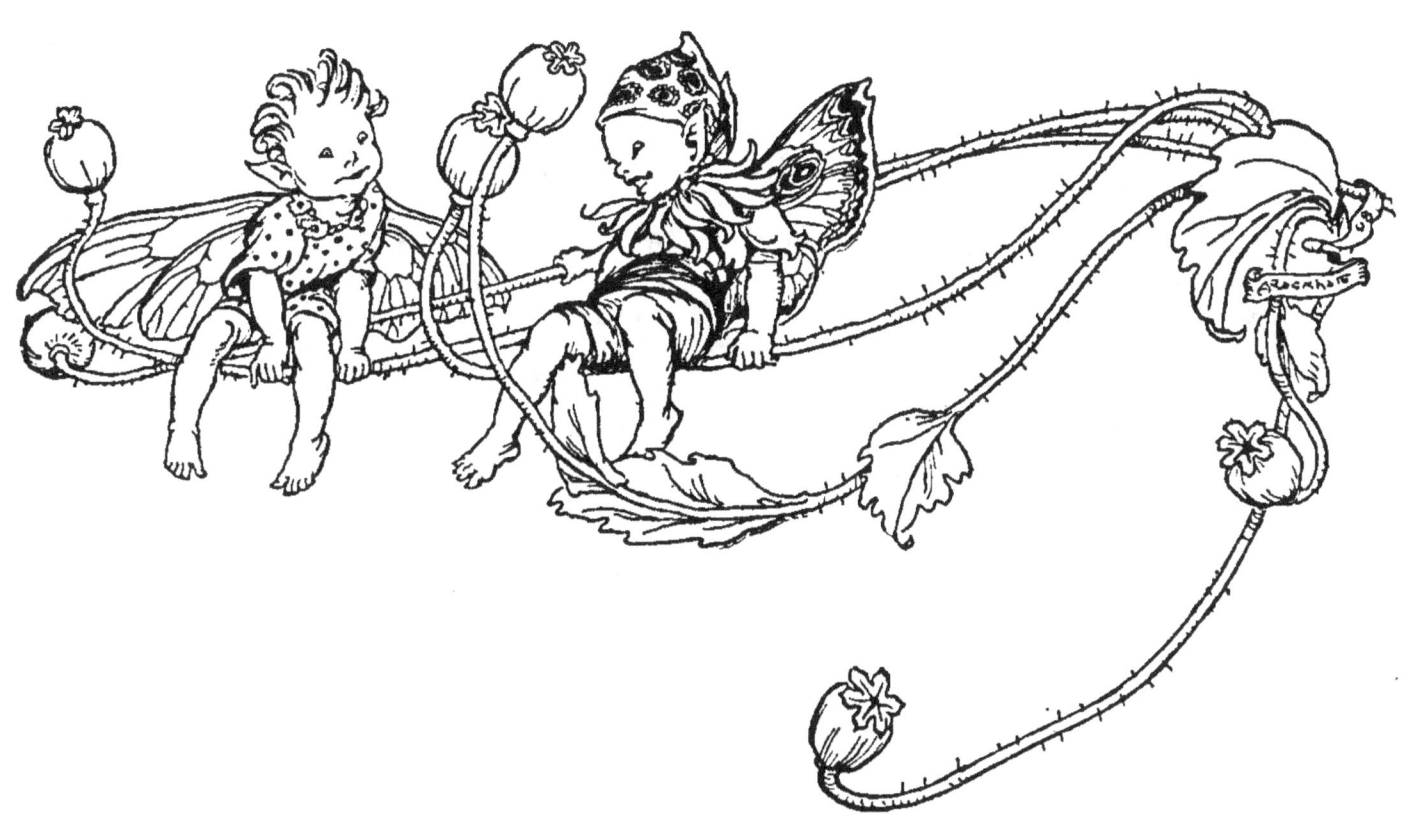

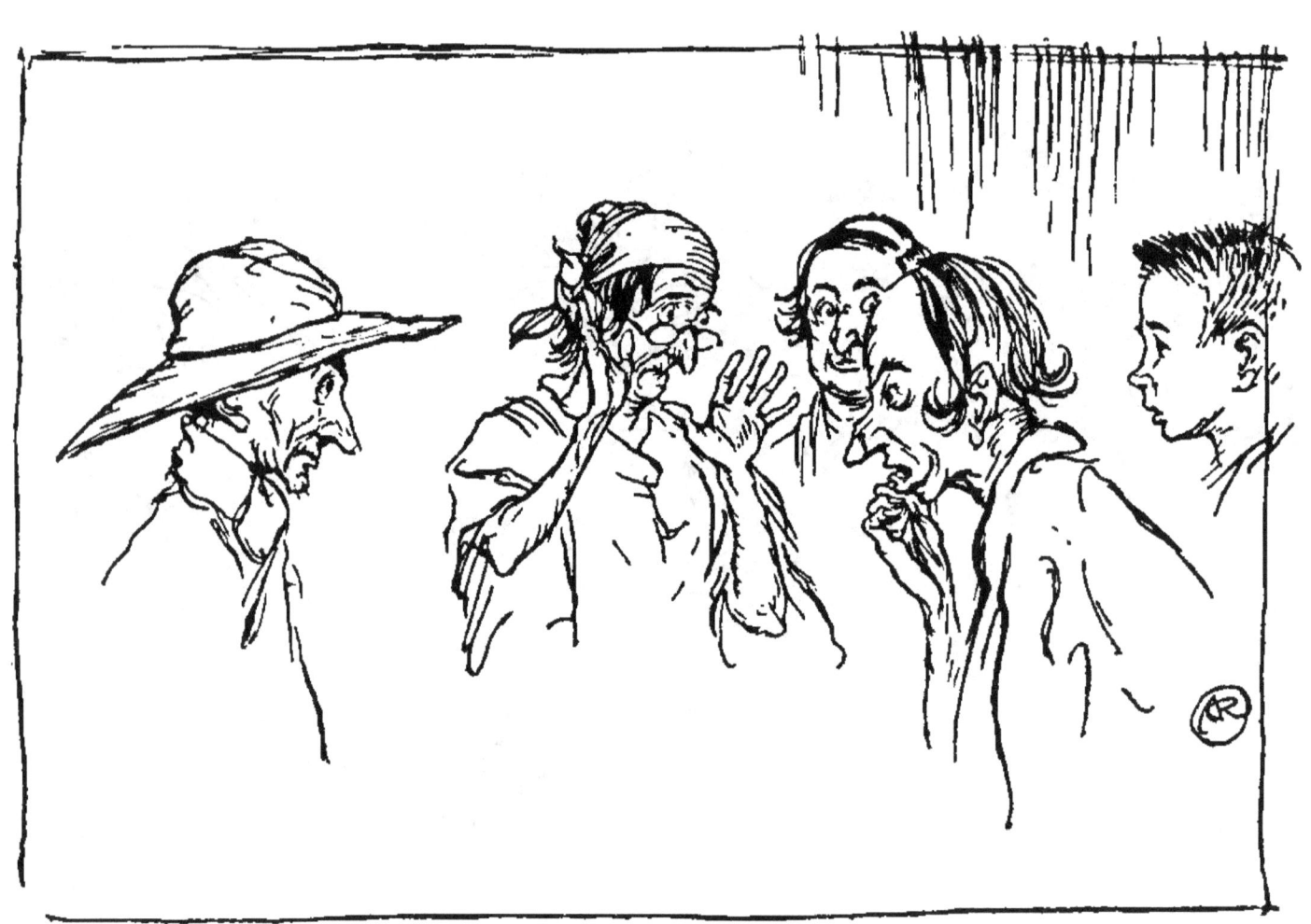

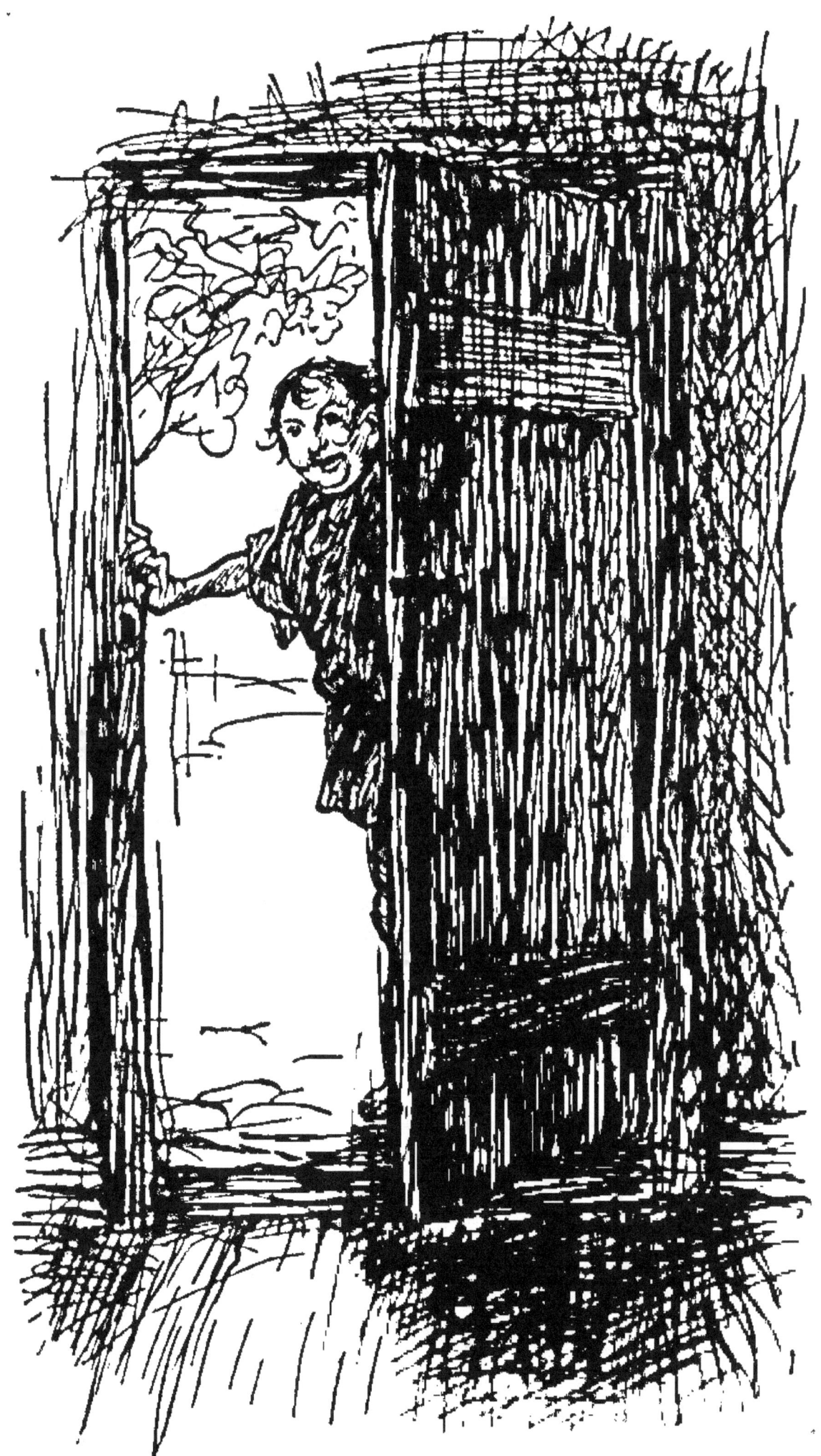

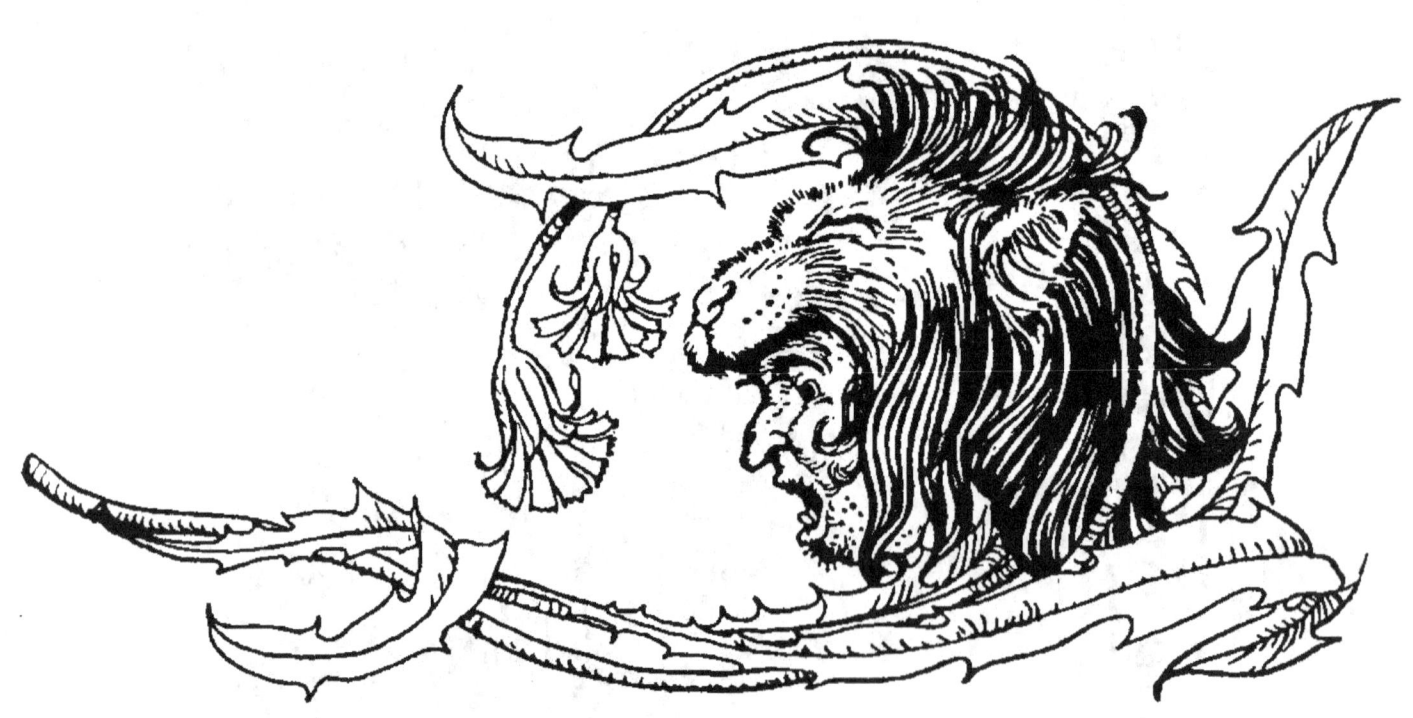

Exit Moonshine.

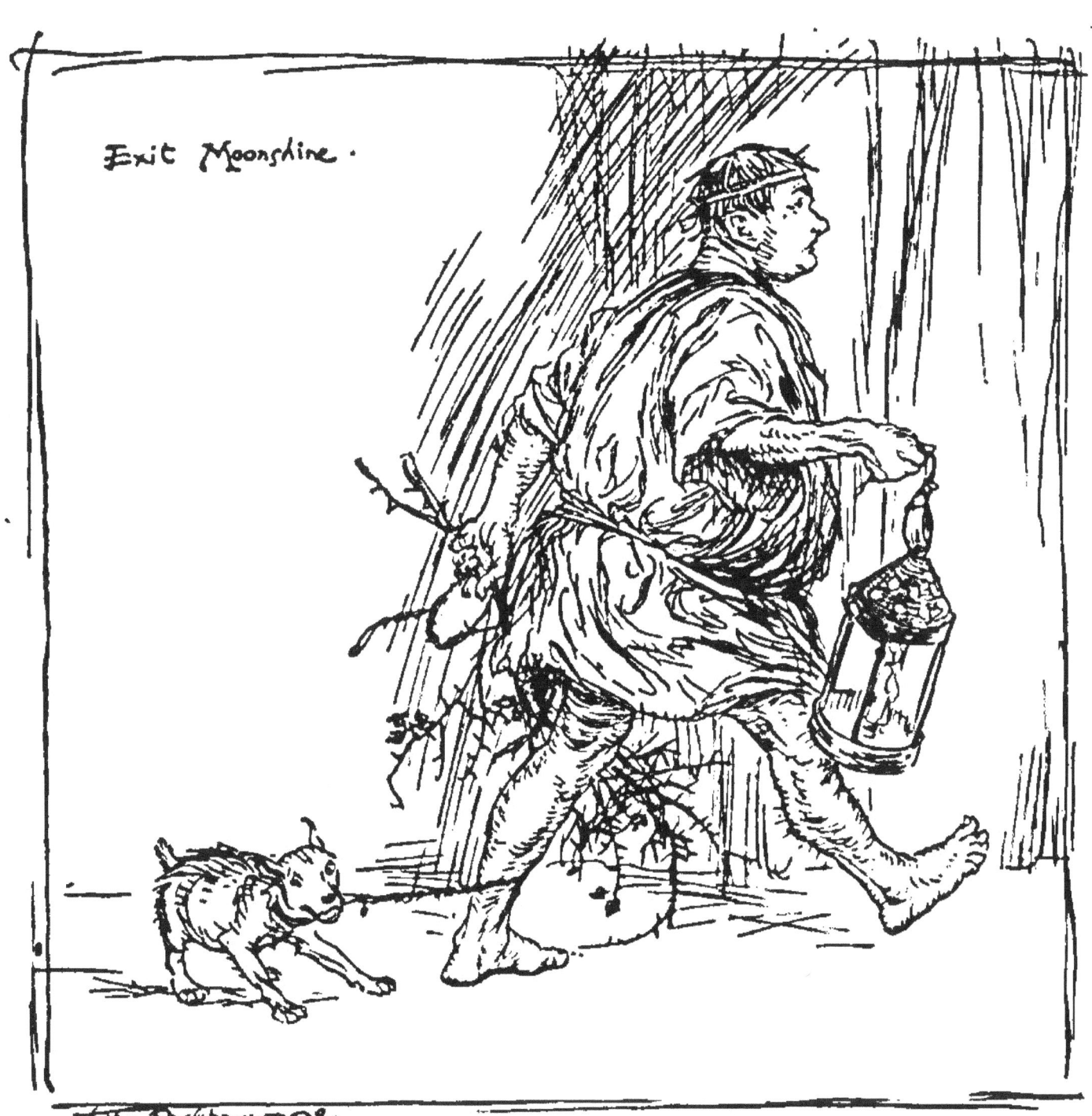